IN REMEMBRANCE OF ME

Meditations for the Season of Lent

Other books by Sheri A. Sutton

And So It Is

The Light of Christmas

In Remembrance of Me

Meditations for the Season of Lent

SHERI A. SUTTON

IN REMEMBRANCE OF ME

Meditations for the Season of Lent

© Sheri A. Sutton 2015

ISBN: 978-0-6925876-9-0

Scriptures taken from THE HOLY BIBLE, NEW INTERNATIONAL VERSION®, NIV®. Copyright © 1973, 1978, 1984, 2011 by Biblica, Inc.® Used by permission. All rights reserved worldwide.

Published by
Sheri A. Sutton
P.O. Box 22
Wichita Falls, Texas 76307
United States of America

www.sheriasutton.com

TABLE OF CONTENTS

We do not live as those who have no hope. For through Jesus Christ, we have the hope of resurrection.

INTRODUCTION

Observed in many Christian churches, Lent begins on Ash Wednesday and ends on Holy Saturday. It is the forty-day period excluding Sundays leading up to Easter in which the institutional purpose of Lent is magnified during Holy Week.

Lent is a season in which we can grow closer to God. To know God, we must first know Jesus, the Son of God and the Son of Man. As we contemplate the life, death, and resurrection of Jesus Christ, *In Remembrance of Me* will focus on the themes of reflection, prayer, repentance, trust, sacrifice, and redemption.

Forty is a significant number in Scripture. A forty-day interval usually represents a period of testing or trial ending with a time of restoration or renewal.

Before the beginning of his ministry, Jesus spent forty days and nights fasting in the wilderness and was hungry according to Scripture. During this time, he was "tempted by the devil" (Matthew 4:1). The devil considered him an easy target as he tempted Jesus with worldly rewards. But during the fasting, the practice of prayer and meditation had strengthened Jesus to overcome the enemy's bait by using God's principles found in Scripture. Consequently, the attempts to lead Jesus astray were unsuccessful.

In today's world, we too are tempted, and we need strength and courage to overcome the enemy's lure of a better life. During the Lenten season, we can turn our focus to the resurrecting power of God working in our lives on a daily basis. In using this forty-day period to strengthen our relationship with God as well as reflecting on the sacrifice that he made on our behalf, we can ready ourselves for the empowering celebration of Easter.

REFLECTION...

deep contemplation

WEDNESDAY OF FIRST WEEK

Psalm 32

You are my hiding place; you will protect me from trouble and surround me with songs of deliverance (v. 7).

In the world today there are all types of protection available to us such as police officers, neighborhood watch programs, emergency medical teams, fire departments, fraud protection programs, and a myriad of other such safeguards. But do we really feel safe? Perhaps some of these municipal departments and programs help us to sleep a little easier at night, but what is our true protection from the everyday struggles and demands of life?

The psalmist believed that our true protection came from our relationship with God. Not only would God protect us from the perils of life, but he would also deliver us from the yoke of our own faults and weaknesses.

Regardless of how unhealthy or devastating our choices have been, God forgives us when we turn to him and acknowledge our wrongdoings. As we begin this season of Lent, let us reflect honestly on our shortcomings and become willing to lay those at Jesus' feet. Most importantly, may we prepare ourselves for God's grace and redemption.

Almighty and gracious God, as I reflect on your power and grace, I know that you will protect me. May you grant me mercy and forgive my faults and weaknesses. Amen.

Thursday of First Week

Psalm 63

You, God, are my God, earnestly I seek you; I thirst for you, my whole being longs for you, in a dry and parched land where there is no water (v. 1).

Severe drought conditions have spread across a large portion of the United States these last few years. Inadequate water supplies have forced us to change our daily management of water and to seek alternative solutions. We have been reminded on a daily basis just how important and sustaining water is to life.

In the psalm above, David confessed of his longing for God. Surrounded by his enemies, he reflected on the power of God and the expectation of his deliverance.

Just as we cannot survive without water, neither can we survive without God's love and protection from the demands of life. God is life. He gives life, and he sustains life. He is our help in time of need and our sustenance when we hunger for satisfaction. Just as the psalmist called on God for deliverance from his enemies, we too can call on God when the deserts of our lives overcome us.

Redeeming God, I hunger and thirst for your presence and help in my life. Transform the deserts of my life into a land filled with the bounty of your love. Amen.

Isaiah 55:1-9

"Why spend money on what is not bread, and your labor on what does not satisfy? Listen, listen to me, and eat what is good, and you will delight in the richest of fare" (v. 2).

Jesus declared to the crowd, "I am the bread of life. Whoever comes to me will never go hungry, and whoever believes in me will never be thirsty" (John 6:35). This is the first of seven "I am" statements that Jesus made. What does it mean?

There is a difference in being full and being satisfied. The crowds following Jesus had experienced the feeding of 5,000 with five loaves of bread and two small fish. They wanted more miracles from Jesus so that they would believe. But how many more miracles would it take for them to truly believe—five, twenty, one hundred? Would being *full* of miracles bring satisfaction?

We do the same today. We want more so that we can feel full. A higher salary will bring security until the company closes without notice. Another relationship will be more fulfilling until the problems begin and you long for something different. A larger house will bring you enjoyment until the monthly payment becomes a burden. The trappings of the world never bring true satisfaction. Only God can give us what we need to feel truly satisfied and fulfilled.

Holy God, fill me with the bread of life so that I may be truly satisfied. Amen.

Philippians 3:4b-14

I want to know Christ—yes, to know the power of his resurrection and participation in his sufferings, becoming like him in his death, and so, somehow, attaining to the resurrection from the dead (vv. 10-11).

For believers everywhere knowing Christ is our goal. But does knowing him only come from reading and studying the Bible? Can we expand our knowledge by reading and studying various theologians or authors who have spent their lives researching and studying Jesus' life, death, and resurrection? Of course, study is important; but there is more.

Paul was sure that the dynamic power for righteous living came through faith in Christ. In the verses above, he expressed his desire to experience the resurrecting power of God through Christ in the present. How do we connect today with that power?

Faith in Christ is a process developed through our daily experiences. Spending time in prayer and meditation on a regular basis strengthens our spirits and opens our minds and hearts to the reality of the living God. As we rely daily on a power beyond ourselves to deliver us from the struggles of life, we will encounter the Son of God as we have never encountered him before.

Almighty and powerful God, I want to know you and recognize you working in my life on a daily basis. Help me to open my mind and my heart to your power and presence. Amen.

PRAYER...

opening one's spirit to God's spirit

Monday of Second Week

Psalm 27

The LORD is the stronghold of my life—of whom shall I be afraid? I remain confident of this: I will see the goodness of the LORD in the land of the living. Wait for the LORD; be strong and take heart and wait for the LORD (vv. 13-14).

Most of us do not like to wait because we want what we want now. We want the traffic light to remain green so that we will not be delayed. We want to be first in line at the grocery store so that we can arrive home in time to watch our favorite TV program. We want the doctor to give us a prescription so that we can lose weight in a week instead of making a lifestyle change. We want everything today!

The reality is that it takes time to get from point A to point B, and it takes time to change. It also takes time to wait for answers to our questions, for resolutions to our problems, and for the achievement of our long-sought-after dreams.

Just like the psalmist, we know that God's timing is not our timing. Through the study of Scripture, we also know that God's timing is perfect and there is a season for everything. Through prayer, we receive the strength and courage necessary to wait on his guidance, direction, and power to be manifested in our lives. As a result, we can experience God's goodness and grace.

Almighty and loving God, teach me to wait for your direction and answers so that I can experience your power and goodness in my life. Amen.

TUESDAY OF SECOND WEEK

Psalm 91

"Because he loves me," says the LORD, "I will rescue him; I will protect him, for he acknowledges my name. He will call on me, and I will answer him; I will be with him in trouble, I will deliver him and honor him. With long life I will satisfy him and show him my salvation" (vv. 14-16).

Psalm 91 begins with "He who dwells in the shelter of the Most High will rest in the shadow of the Almighty" (v. 1). It is a striking image especially against other images that we may see on television or at the movies. Think about it. How would you feel sheltered by the shadow of God—protected, loved, satisfied?

For many, life is full of struggle, pain, and doubt. We may feel abandoned or cast out. Perhaps we seek ways to resolve the battles of life through our own power only to be disappointed and discouraged when answers and solutions are not readily available. But for those who believe in the power of God, we are resurrected from the pit of despair and hopelessness.

God loves us without question. And when we acknowledge his presence and purpose in our lives, there is nothing he will not do for us. He will hear our cries and answer us, protect us, deliver us, respect us, and fulfill us. The psalmist knew God loved him, but more importantly he loved God. And because he did, he claimed God's promises with confidence and assurance. We can do the same.

Almighty God, I acknowledge you as my Redeemer. I trust that you will protect me, deliver me, and honor me all the days of my life. Amen.

Psalm 118

You are my God, and I will praise you; you are my God, and I will exalt you. Give thanks to the LORD, for he is good; is love endures forever (vv. 28-29).

Love is a powerful force. It brings people together, builds relationships or restores them, heals our spirits, and forgives our many shortcomings and mistakes. It changes the outcome of a situation and transforms our lives. Love is God's power at work.

But for many, love has strings attached or conditions of required behavior. We may be told that we are loved only to discover that love carries impossible requirements. We may be told that we are loved only to be treated in such a way that damages our spirits. God's love, however, is authentic. His love is truth, and his love is forever.

We may wonder how God can love us so much, especially if we have fallen short of God's glory. But we are his creation and made in his image. We are of value to him. Even in our darkest moments, we can reach out to God. We can lay the broken pieces of our lives at his feet and experience his unconditional love—his everlasting, eternal, and enduring love.

Loving God, I pray with gratitude and humbly accept your redeeming and merciful love. Amen.

THURSDAY OF SECOND WEEK

Luke 4:1-13

Jesus, full of the Holy Spirit, left the Jordan and was led by the Spirit into the wilderness, where for forty days he was tempted by the devil. He ate nothing during those days, and at the end of them he was hungry (vv. 1-2).

We can only imagine what Jesus must have experienced in the Judean wilderness for forty days and nights. The desert landscape was mostly uninhabitable with scorching hot days and extremely cold nights. Wild animals roamed the land, and food and water were scarce.

According to the verses above, Jesus fasted during his time in the wilderness. Most usually, fasting is a practice of abstinence from food and/or water for a specified period of time while focusing on prayer. Fasting shifts our focus to God instead of the world around us, thus creating a transformation within us.

This time in the wilderness strengthened Jesus, and as a result the devil's temptations had no power. He returned to Galilee, empowered by the Spirit, and began his ministry. Many times over the next three years, Jesus left the crowds and went alone to commune with the Father. It was where he found his strength, and it is where we can find ours.

Gracious heavenly Father, I hunger to spend time alone with you. Help me to find strength in you. Amen.

FRIDAY OF SECOND WEEK

Hebrews 12:1-3

Therefore, since we are surrounded by such a great cloud of witnesses, let us throw off everything that hinders and the sin that so easily entangles. And let us run with perseverance the race marked out for us, fixing our eyes on Jesus, the pioneer and perfecter of faith (vv. 1-2).

One definition for perseverance is a continued steady course of action in spite of difficulties. As believers, our goal is to focus on our objective—a relationship with God through our faith in Jesus Christ. Regardless of the struggles we may face, our faith empowers us to overcome our doubts and fears.

Life is not easy. In fact, on many days it is unbearable. A loved one dies, and we are left alone. The doctor says its cancer, and we fear the consequences. At the age of sixty, we are unemployed with no hope of another job. Life seems hopeless, and we feel alone and afraid.

Through our faith in Jesus Christ, the Son of the Living God, we can persevere even in the middle of life's most challenging and difficult moments. Cling to his words of truth and power. Stand on his promises of forgiveness and redemption. And believe that through him all things are possible.

God of power and strength, empower me to persevere even in the midst of struggle and disappointment. Help me to keep my focus on you. Amen.

SATURDAY OF SECOND WEEK

1 Corinthians 10:1-13

No temptation has overtaken you except what is common to mankind. And God is faithful; he will not let you be tempted beyond what you can bear. But when you are tempted, he will also provide a way out so that you can endure it (v. 13).

Temptation in and of itself is not sinful. Yielding to it is. We are often enticed, coaxed, or persuaded to do something very ordinary or familiar. We may engage in gossip of a co-worker and not realize the devastating result to his reputation. Perhaps, we have financial problems and justify taking money from the petty cash fund as a temporary solution. Seemingly innocent situations cause pain and hurt to ourselves as well as to others.

When we are faced with struggles in our lives, there is a solution—claiming God's power to keep us from temptation. In the Lord's Prayer it states, "And lead us not into temptation, but deliver us from the evil one" (Matthew 6:13). God's power breaks the yoke of temptation so that we can be the person that he created us to be.

Through God's power, we are empowered to stand up, to be men and women of character and integrity, and to be honorable even in the midst of ungodliness. God calls us to do what is right, and with his provision we can.

Almighty God, strengthen my relationship with you through prayer so that I may stand strong against the temptations of life. Amen.

REPENTANCE...

*the admission of one's wrongdoings
and the resolve to change*

Psalm 31

Into your hands I commit my spirit; deliver me, LORD, my faithful God (v. 5).

Humility is often misunderstood. Many think it means humiliation. Quite the opposite, it is surrender. We all do it. We try to manage and control our lives as well as the lives of others. We think that our power is all we have to work through daily struggles, to confront life-changing events, and to obtain our dreams and desires. But there is a power beyond any human power at work in our lives.

Entering into a committed relationship with God requires the surrender of our total self into his hands. The psalmist believed "Since you are my rock and my fortress, for the sake of your name lead me and guide me" (v. 3). When we give our lives to God, we are relinquishing any preconceived ideas, attitudes, and misplaced control for his power. We are exposing our weaknesses so that his strength is revealed.

It is through his power that we are called to his purpose. It is through his power that we are strengthened to complete the task. And it is through his power that we are transformed.

Most powerful God, I surrender myself to you so that you can fill me with your power to accomplish your purpose in my life. Amen.

Psalm 32

Then I acknowledged my sin to you and did not cover up my iniquity. I said, "I will confess my transgressions to the LORD." And you forgave the guilt of my sin (v. 5).

It has been said that confession is good for the soul. And indeed it is. One meaning for confession is an admission of guilt for a wrongdoing. It has been proven that feelings of guilt and shame if allowed to fester harm a person physically, emotionally, and spiritually.

At the beginning of Jesus' ministry as recorded in Matthew 4:17, he said, "Repent, for the kingdom of heaven has come near." Repentance is the admission of one's shortcomings and the desire to change one's thinking and behavior. It is never easy to admit that we are at fault and have committed some type of wrongdoing. However, to move forward in a relationship with God, admitting our shortcomings is exactly what we need to do.

As we humble ourselves before the Creator of the universe and all therein, we are filled with God's resurrecting power to move forward in the rebuilding of our lives. He walks with us, forgives us, and strengthens us so that we can be all that he created us to be.

My Creator and Redeemer, I admit my wrongdoings and ask for your forgiveness and power to rebuild my life. Amen.

Psalm 51:1-9

Have mercy on me, O God, according to your unfailing love; according to your great compassion blot out my transgressions. Wash away all my iniquity and cleanse me from my sin (vv. 1-2).

Have you ever been dirty from head to toe? Perhaps you worked in the yard all day planting a garden or flower beds. You dug dirt and moved dirt. You leveled the beds, tilled the garden rows, and dug holes for plants. You labored all day to finish your project, and now you are covered in dirt and sweat.

The only thing you want to do is jump into the shower. As the dirt and sweat wash away from your body, you feel clean, fresh, and new. And so it is for us when we come into a relationship with God.

As we come to know God, we start over. When we humbly and genuinely admit our shortcomings, God forgives us. Through the blood of Christ, we are made clean and brought into the light of God's mercy and grace. From the messiness of our lives, God creates and transforms so that we can experience the newness of a God-filled life.

Holy and merciful God, transform the messiness of my life into something new and vibrant filled with your love and grace. Amen.

Psalm 51:10-19

Create in me a pure heart, O God, and renew a steadfast spirit within me (v. 10).

Steadfast is defined as being firm in belief, determined, or loyal. When we have a steadfast spirit, we stand firm in our faith regardless of the circumstances because we know with certainty that God is with us.

In Psalm 51, David humbly prayed for forgiveness and cleansing from his unhealthy choices and shortcomings that separated him from God. He was sure that God would bring him out of the darkness of despair and shame into the light of grace.

All of us make unhealthy choices in our lives at one time or another and fall short of God's glory. But God is faithful and merciful. He loves us in spite of ourselves, he forgives our failures, and he celebrates our willingness to try again. Just like David, we can be sure that through a steadfast relationship with God we too will be restored to wholeness.

Holy God, remove in me all that stands in my way of having a steadfast spirit so that I can be restored to wholeness. Amen.

FRIDAY OF THIRD WEEK

Joel 2:12-17

"Even now," declares the LORD, "return to me with all your heart, with fasting and weeping and mourning" (v. 12).

How many times do we fall into the trap of being severed from God? We believe that we are not good enough, or obedient enough, or important enough for God's interest in our lives. And so we take a familiar road of isolation and separation. The struggles of life become agonizing and threatening, and we feel lost and alone. We want to call out to God, but we are embarrassed and afraid. How can he forgive us, or love us, or want us?

Jesus spoke of a shepherd who left his herd of sheep to find the one lost sheep. When the shepherd found the sheep, he rejoiced. In our relationship with God, he is the shepherd who searches for us when we are lost. Regardless of the severity of our shortcomings or errors in judgment, God rejoices when we return to him with a repentant heart. It may not be easy to admit our failures, but God is ready and willing to take us back into the fold.

Almighty God, the Shepherd of my life, I come to you with a repentant heart. Renew my spirit so that my life will be a testament to your love and grace. Amen.

Saturday of Third Week

John 13:21-38

Then Jesus answered, "Will you really lay down your life for me? Very truly I tell you, before the rooster crows, you will disown me three times" (v. 38)!

It is interesting to speculate what went through Peter's mind on that fateful night when he denied knowing Jesus three times. Was he disillusioned with his response? Was he filled with anguish and despair? Was he surprised that Jesus knew all along what he would do?

We will never know, but we do know what we feel when we deny our beliefs—ashamed, guilt-ridden, and tormented. It is not easy to live a God-centered life in today's world. Many are persecuted for their beliefs. Some are ridiculed or bullied, and it may seem less confrontational to say nothing. At some point in our lives, however, we all come to a crossroad that demands we stand up for our beliefs.

When we take our fears to God and humbly ask for his strength and grace, he gives us the power we need to face the adversities and roadblocks in our lives. God is greater than our difficulties. God is greater than our fears. And God is greater than our failures. During this Lenten season, let us renew our resolve to be more centered in our relationship with the God who loves us, protects us, and honors our willingness to stand firmly on our faith in him.

Gracious God, I humble myself before you and ask you to renew my spirit so that I will not waiver in my faith in you. Amen.

TRUST...

assured reliance on a power beyond ourselves

MONDAY OF FOURTH WEEK

Psalm 27

The LORD is my light and my salvation—whom shall I fear (v. 1)?

It is easy to feel afraid in today's world. There is hunger, persecution, greed, and war. Many are tired and weary and suffer from exhaustion and despair. So what do we do when the world overpowers us?

If we believe and trust in the resurrecting power of God, then fear serves no purpose. It only defeats us. When we see the struggles of life through the eyes of God's truth, we are delivered from the yoke of fear.

The psalmist knew without doubt that he could put his hope in God to relinquish his fear. He knew without question that God was ever present and ever ready to deliver him from harm. And God wants to deliver us as well. He is here, in this moment, standing guard. He is our light in the darkness of life and our stronghold in the midst of adversity. Through his power and strength, our fears are conquered. At last, we have no reason to be afraid.

Almighty God, my light and salvation, I come to you because I know and trust that your resurrecting power can overcome my fears. Deliver me out of the darkness of life into your eternal light. Amen.

TUESDAY OF FOURTH WEEK

Psalm 31

But I trust in you, LORD; I say, "You are my God." My times are in your hands; deliver me from the hands of my enemies, from those who pursue me. Let your face shine on your servant; save me in your unfailing love (vv.14-16).

When we come to God, trust is paramount in building our relationship. The aspects of trust include reliance, confident expectation, certainty, and hope.

Trust may be difficult to comprehend in today's world. Politicians run for office asking the voters to trust their ideas for a better world. Once elected, their ideas fall short. Two people pledge their love to one another and trust that their marriage will last for a lifetime. Many times marriages fail, and hearts are broken. A business grows and hires many employees who trust on their monthly income to support a family. After many years, the company closes with no explanation and leaves its employees without a way to survive.

We often put our trust in those who cannot be trusted, which results in not trusting at all. Scripture tells us over and over again that we can trust God. We can bring him our struggles, our disappointments, our failures, and our weaknesses. He will not abandon us, or disown us, or betray us. He will deliver us, shelter us, and surround us with his unfailing love.

Loving God, I give you my life with the assurance that you will deliver me and love me for all eternity. Amen.

Wednesday of Fourth Week

Psalm 71

As for me, I will always have hope; I will praise you more and more. My mouth will tell of your righteous deeds, of your saving acts all day long—though I know not how to relate them all. I will come and proclaim your mighty acts, Sovereign LORD; I will proclaim your righteous deeds, yours alone (vv. 14-16).

The psalmist knew that there was always hope. He also knew to present his requests for help with anticipation of God's deliverance. He was certain of God's unfailing love, mercy, and grace.

Hope is that spark deep within our spirits that propels us forward even in the midst of struggle and pain. It is that still small voice inside that tells us that all is not lost and that there are possibilities that we have yet to consider.

Hope fuels healing, change, and transformation. At any moment the power of God as witnessed through the resurrection of Jesus Christ can transform our lives. When we are dead in spirit, that power can renew us and raise us from the tomb of sorrow and misery into the light of the living God.

God of hope and possibility, I ask for your deliverance from my struggles and will declare your unfailing mercy and grace. Amen.

THURSDAY OF FOURTH WEEK

Psalm 91

Whoever dwells in the shelter of the Most High will rest in the shadow of the Almighty. I will say of the LORD, "He is my refuge and my fortress, my God, in whom I trust" (vv. 1-2).

"In God We Trust" became mandatory on all U.S. coin and currency in 1955 and the official U.S. motto in 1956. For a country with its roots in religious freedom, "In God We Trust" spoke to its foundational beliefs.

For the psalmist, his foundation was also rooted in his belief of God as his source and deliverer. No matter what enemies stood before him, he was unafraid. God would hear his cries for help and would answer. The psalmist did not doubt. He knew God was more powerful than any enemy, seen or unseen.

Today, many are persecuted, bullied, or unaccepted for their beliefs. There are accusations, destruction of property, and lawsuits if we dare to stand and voice our reliance in a power greater than ourselves. But God's covenant to each of us who believe is unfailing and never-ending. He will be our refuge and fortress in the midst of our struggles because we can trust him.

Almighty God, I trust in your sovereignty and your power to protect me and strengthen me in the midst of my daily struggles. Amen.

FRIDAY OF FOURTH WEEK

Psalm 116

I love the LORD, for he heard my voice; he heard my cry for mercy. Because he turned his ear to me, I will call on him as long as I live (vv. 1-2).

We all want to live a long and healthy life. For many of us, death is many years away. For some, death may be closer than we want. Regardless of how long we live, life is too short.

Jesus came to give us life. When he was resurrected from the tomb, he disarmed everything of this world that claims authority over humanity—even death. The psalmist cried out to be delivered from death. God heard him and saved him. God will do the same for us.

When we come into a relationship with God, we die to our old selves and are born to a new life. "For you, LORD, have delivered me from death, my eyes from tears, my feet from stumbling, that I may walk before the LORD in the land of the living" (vv. 8-9).

Merciful God, I call out to you to save me and know with certainty that you hear me. Amen.

SATURDAY OF FOURTH WEEK

Lamentations 3:1-9, 19-24

Because of the LORD's great love we are not consumed, for his compassions never fail. They are new every morning; great is your faithfulness. I say to myself, "The LORD is my portion; therefore I will wait for him" (vv. 22-24).

The book of Lamentations is a book of laments, which are passionate expressions of grief and sorrow. However, it is also a book of hope and trust. Chapter 3:21 is the theological highpoint of the book. It states, "Yet this I call to mind and therefore I have hope." Even in the midst of gut-wrenching grief and sorrow, the writer trusted God's faithfulness. And where there is trust, there is hope.

Picture your life. More than likely it has been filled with moments of happiness and moments of great sadness and despair. Often life's difficulties throw us into such deep darkness that we may think we will never be lifted up again. But God is faithful beyond measure. He has promised to remain with us, to love us, and to loosen the chains that bind us.

Out of the darkest moments of our lives, God's resurrecting power can raise us into the light. The writer of Lamentations knew that he could trust God, and in that trust he found hope. We can do the same.

Gracious God, I bring you the darkest moments of my life. I trust your faithfulness and hope in your redeeming power to bring me back into the light. Amen.

JESUS...

the Son of the Living God

MONDAY OF FIFTH WEEK

Isaiah 42:1-9

Here is my servant, whom I uphold, my chosen one in whom I delight; I will put my Spirit on him, and he will bring justice to the nations (v. 1).

The servant theme is an important one in the book of Isaiah. As seen in verses one through nine, Isaiah's portrayal of the servant emphasizes his gentleness, and in the verse above the servant points us to the Messiah. As revealed through Jesus Christ, the mission of the Messiah is one of redemption of the lost and discarded.

On a night long ago God entered the world. He came with no fanfare and no headline in the daily newspaper. His parents were not interviewed by reporters, nor did they sign a contract for a reality television program. The only sign that the Messiah had entered the world was a star that shone brightly in the heavens.

Jesus comes to us today in much the same way—quietly and with purpose. He calls us to leave our brokenness behind and follow him into a new life. He calls us to love one another as he loves us. He calls us to forgive one another as he forgives us. And he calls us to serve others as he serves us. It is a simple message that has moved beyond the restrictions of time and space and still calls us today.

Gracious God, you came into this world to redeem me and call me for your purpose. Open my mind and heart so that I may be the person that you created me to be. Amen.

Luke 9:28-36

As he was praying, the appearance of his face changed, and his clothes became as bright as a flash of lightning (v. 29).

Jesus and three of his disciples went on the mountain. Moses and Elijah appeared and spoke with Jesus about his coming task—delivering his people from the pit of darkness and bringing them into the light of God.

Although the disciples were close, they were drowsy and not completely aware of the circumstances. When they became fully awake, Peter said to Jesus, "Let us put up three shelters" (v. 33). Without doubt, he did not fully comprehend the situation. Jesus had a purpose to fulfill in his few remaining days and did not have time to remain on the mountain.

We can be very much like the disciples—unaware. The disciples had been given a glimpse into eternity and did not know it. During this Lenten season, let us become more aware of God moving in us and through us. Let us become more aware of God's purpose for our lives. And let us prepare ourselves for the resurrecting power of God that brings us out of the darkness into the eternal light.

Almighty God, open my eyes so that I can see your presence in my life and bring me out of the darkness into your eternal light. Amen.

John 12:1-8

"Leave her alone," Jesus replied. "It was intended that she should save this perfume for the day of my burial. You will always have the poor among you, but you will not always have me" (vv. 7-8).

Most of us can admit that we never fully appreciate those we love until they are no longer here. It is curious that we take so much for granted when life is always full of interruptions, changes, and losses.

Jesus had journeyed to Bethany a few days before the Passover, and a dinner was held in his honor at the home of Lazarus. During the festivities, Mary anointed his feet with an expensive perfume. One of the disciples questioned Jesus about the costly oil. Why was it not sold and used to help the poor?

The disciples still did not realize the pain and loss they would experience. Nor did they understand that Jesus' purpose was soon to be fulfilled on a cross. They were still focused on life with Jesus as they knew it.

During this season of reflection and prayer, let us stay mindful that life is not destined to stay the same. Life is ever changing and fluid. However, life is also full of endless opportunities to love and acknowledge those who are important to us. Let us not miss the chance to do so.

God of love and light, help me to be aware of and acknowledge those I love while I still have the chance to do so. Amen.

Philippians 2:5-8

And being found in appearance as a man, he humbled himself by becoming obedient to death—even death on a cross (v. 8)!

Jesus, who was the very essence of God, humbled himself by laying aside his glory to take on the nature of a servant. He came to earth to walk among us, to teach us about God's unique relationship with man, and to free us from the yoke of slavery. On a cross, he was crucified, cursed, and bore the weight of humanity's transgressions for all time.

Many have questioned the authenticity of Jesus' selfless act of redemption. Was it real or contrived? Why would God, the Creator of the world and all therein, go through such a dramatic display for a seemingly fallen world?

It is difficult to comprehend the depth of love that God has for his creation. When God created man, he wove us from the depths of earth and breathed into us the very breath of life. He magnificently created us in his image and ordained our days. Through the life, death, and resurrection of Jesus Christ, he secured our eternal destiny by shattering the chains of death and releasing us from the bondage of our own self-will. "For God did not send his Son into the world to condemn the world, but to save the world through him" (John 3:17).

Merciful God, may I manifest your glory through obedience to all that you call me to do. Amen.

Philippians 2:9-11

Therefore God exalted him to the highest place and gave him the name that is above every name... (v. 9).

There is power in a name. A name gives authority, identification, and recognition. Most of us like to be called by our name. It validates and proclaims our existence. There are also names that injure us and hold us captive. Those names can prevent us from being who God created us to be.

According to Scripture, there is one name above all others—Jesus. It is comforting to our spirits and calms our minds. It can deliver us from unhealthy lifestyles, the darkness of grief, the despair of loneliness, and the trap of anger and resentment. It can heal our bodies, minds, and spirits. By repeating it often, it will bring us peace and offer us hope.

Jesus, the name that identifies the resurrecting power of God, is more powerful than any other name. If we let it permeate our hearts and occupy our minds, we will know its power—Jesus, the name above all others.

Holy God, when I am alone, afraid, or full of despair, remind me of your resurrecting power that is found in your Son, Jesus Christ. Amen.

Hebrews 4:14-16

For we do not have a high priest who is unable to empathize with our weaknesses, but we have one who has been tempted in every way, just as we are—yet he did not sin. Let us then approach God's throne of grace with confidence, so that we may receive mercy and find grace to help us in our time of need (vv. 15-16).

In our quest to live a righteous life, God sets the bar high and gives us Jesus as an example. Although he lived without sin, Jesus knew hunger, despair, abandonment, grief, and pain. He identified with man's suffering; yet he knew the resurrecting power of God.

We too can know that power. The power that broke the chains of death and raised Jesus from the tomb is still available to us today. It can raise us from the depths of despair, release us from the chains of our self-will, and free us to be the people that God created us to be.

God honors our willingness to live a godly life. When we come to him through our faith and belief in Jesus, the Christ, he pours upon us his mercy and grace and forgives our wrongdoings. He fills us with his love; and in that moment, we are redeemed for all eternity.

Gracious and merciful God, through my faith in Jesus Christ, I lay before you my transgressions and ask for your abundant mercy and grace. Amen.

SACRIFICE...

something of value given for a higher purpose

MONDAY OF SIXTH WEEK

Psalm 22

Dogs surround me, a pack of villains encircles me; they pierce my hands and my feet. All my bones are on display; people stare and gloat over me. They divide my clothes among them and cast lots for my garment (vv. 16-18).

In the psalm listed above, David cried out as the righteous sufferer and prayed in anguish for God to deliver him from his enemies. This psalm is quoted frequently in the New Testament and is a prelude to the crucifixion of Jesus Christ.

Jesus was surrounded by those who were afraid of his message and wanted to kill him. When he was crucified, his accusers cursed and ridiculed him. As he hung on the cross, lots were cast for his robe. Jesus indeed became the righteous sufferer for all mankind.

Many of us have struggles and hardships that seem unbearable. How can we overcome when all seems lost? When Jesus took our transgressions to the depths of darkness and returned in the fullness of everlasting light, he gave us the solution to dispel the darkness in our own lives.

During this season of Lent, let us concentrate on the resurrecting power of God that is available to all of us. May we tap into that power so that we may no longer walk in fear of the darkness but walk in the freedom of God's everlasting light.

Almighty God, may your resurrecting power surround me and keep me from harm so that I may walk in your light today and always. Amen.

TUESDAY OF SIXTH WEEK

Luke 23:1-12

Then the whole assembly rose and led him off to Pilate. And they began to accuse him, saying, "We have found this man subverting our nation. He opposes payment of taxes to Caesar and claims to be Messiah, a king" (vv. 1-2).

Most of us have been judged at one time or another. Perhaps, we have different values and standards than those around us. Maybe, we have diverse views concerning the world situation. If we are different in any way in comparison to our family, friends, or co-workers, we more than likely have been criticized for our beliefs, our attitudes, or our actions.

Jesus was persecuted by those who did not understand his ministry and was falsely accused, ridiculed, and crucified. Many thought that was the end of the story. But for believers everywhere, we know that was only the beginning.

Jesus overcame the judgment of those around him because his objective went far beyond the ideas and perceptions of his time. His purpose was eternal; and as witnessed through his resurrection, his power was undeniable.

Judgment is very often based on opinion and not factual information. Perhaps, we need to take a second look at those around us and see beyond the world's standards. Maybe, God's purpose is being fulfilled right in front of our eyes.

Holy God, please deliver me from the character defect of judgment so that I may see you at work in those around me. Amen.

WEDNESDAY OF SIXTH WEEK

Luke 23:13-25

But with loud shouts they insistently demanded that he be crucified, and their shouts prevailed. So Pilate decided to grant their demand. He released the man who had been thrown into prison for insurrection and murder, the one they asked for, and surrendered Jesus to their will (vv. 23-25).

We never know when we may have to make a life-altering decision. Will we be able to analyze all the facts and determine the best outcome for ourselves and others? Life is not easy, and many times we are thrown into a situation that is unexpected.

The leaders of the governing body led Jesus to Pilate for sentencing. After examining the list of charges, Pilate could find no reason to crucify Jesus; but the crowds that had gathered were adamant. "Crucify him," they chanted. Although Pilate did not believe that Jesus was guilty of the charges, he caved under pressure and complied with the mob. Pilate did not know the impact of his decision, nor did he know the part he played in bringing to fruition God's plan for redemption.

We all face situations that call us to make an informed decision that many times can change the course of our lives. During this season of Lent, let us strengthen our minds and hearts so that we can make proper assessments which lead to appropriate decisions. Then, we can take the right action that is needed.

Almighty God, open my mind and heart to your guidance so that I can make appropriate decisions in my life. Amen.

Luke 23:26-49

Two other men, both criminals, were also led out with him to be executed. When they came to the place called the Skull, they crucified him there, along with the criminals—one on his right, the other on his left (vv. 32-33).

Imagine Jesus walking the road to Golgotha—beaten and bloody, carrying the cross. He stumbles and falls. Many people along the way are wailing and moaning because of the torture dispensed on this man from Nazareth, and many ridicule him because he claims to be the Son of God. He drags the cross, his feet barely moving, and slowly walks up the hill.

Life is full of circumstances that knock us to our knees, weight us down, and kill our spirits one step at a time. We often carry guilt, shame, and remorse for our shortcomings. We may have been overcome by grief, stress, and illness. And we may have walked in the darkness of despair, helplessness, and hopelessness. We have carried our own unique cross and walked the road to Golgotha.

When Jesus was crucified, he took all the burdens of the world, all our sins and shortcomings, and all the despair and anguish of our lives to the depths of darkness and returned in the fullness of light and glory. The walk to Golgotha is finished, and for every believer the walk of hope begins.

Merciful God, I pray to remember the great sacrifice that Jesus made for me as he carried the cross and the hope that you give me today through your resurrecting power. Amen.

FRIDAY OF SIXTH WEEK

Hebrews 9:11-15

But when Christ came as high priest of the good things that are now already here, he went through the greater and more perfect tabernacle that is not made with human hands, that is to say, is not a part of this creation. He did not enter by means of the blood of goats and calves; but he entered the Most Holy Place once for all by his own blood, thus obtaining eternal redemption (vv. 11-12).

Sacrifice means to give something of value for a greater purpose. We all give of our time, talents, and financial resources for the greater good of those in need. Jesus was the example of giving to the downcast, the disheartened, and the hungry. But Jesus gave more than that—he gave himself for the salvation of mankind.

Jesus came to share with us about God's faithfulness and enduring love. He came to teach us about community and how to apply God's commandments to our everyday lives. Most importantly, he came to give us everlasting life by losing his.

It is difficult to imagine the sacrifice that Jesus made on our behalf. For centuries, people made animal sacrifices to God to temporarily cover their sins. On the cross, Jesus gave his blood for the eternal redemption of all mankind—the perfect and complete sacrifice.

Redeeming God, I am awed by Jesus' sacrifice for me so that my sins are forgiven by your mercy and grace. Amen.

SATURDAY OF SIXTH WEEK

Hebrews 10:16-25

Then he adds: "Their sins and lawless acts I will remember no more." And where these have been forgiven, sacrifice for sin is no longer necessary (vv. 17-18).

Guilt is a powerful tool that the enemy uses to discourage and confuse us. It persuades us to quit before we reach our goal. It eliminates our desire to better ourselves. Most importantly, it convinces us that God does not love or forgive us. But God does love us, and the depth of that love is immeasurable.

High on a cross centuries ago, all of humanity's ugliness hung between death and life. In that eternal moment, the glory of God overcame. As a result, we are forgiven, redeemed, and transformed.

Where there was despair, now there is hope. Where there was fear, now there is love. And where there was death, now there is life—eternal life in the presence of God surrounded by his unconditional and transforming love.

God of love, light, and life, I am filled with tremendous gratitude for the depth of your love for me. Amen.

REDEMPTION...

being set free

Isaiah 52:13-53:12

But he was pierced for our transgressions, he was crushed for our iniquities; the punishment that brought us peace was on him, and by his wounds we are healed (53:5).

The entire scripture reading referenced above is recognized as one of the clearest and most specific Old Testament illustrations of Christ. Throughout this passage, his suffering and death are prophetically expressed and explained. This passage is most often titled "The Suffering Servant." As we begin Holy Week, let us meditate on the meaning of this passage for us today.

For many believers, Christmas and Easter are the two most important religious holidays. In fact, many go straight from celebrating the birth of Christ to celebrating his resurrection. But there is so much more to the disclosure of the Son of God and the Son of Man to all of humanity.

During Jesus' ministry, he showed us God up close and personal. He revealed God's love for all of us, especially those abused, neglected, and marginalized. He shared with us the principles of humility, generosity, and forgiveness. Finally, he revealed God's plan of redemption. Nailed to a cross, he bore the weight of our transgressions; and in that moment we were healed by God's mercy and grace.

Almighty God, give me a deeper awareness of the life, death, and resurrection of Jesus Christ. Amen.

Luke 23:1-49

Jesus called out with a loud voice, "Father, into your hands I commit my spirit." When he had said this, he breathed his last (v. 46).

There must have been a stark silence among the witnesses of the crucifixion as darkness shrouded the cross, and Jesus breathed his last breath. He did not struggle, nor did he try to undo the inevitable. His purpose was sure, and his commitment was strong.

It is a lesson for each of us. When we find ourselves in the midst of struggle and despair, we can commit our spirits to God. He will comfort us, strengthen us, and heal us. He will walk with us through the valleys of darkness and lead us to the path of peace.

On that fateful day at the hour of death, the temple curtain tore and opened access to God for all mankind. Through the new covenant as proclaimed through the broken body and shed blood of Christ, we are called by faith to receive the inheritance of eternal life.

Most Holy God, I commit my life to you. Lead me on the path of faith and teach me your ways. In the name of Jesus, the Christ, Amen.

John 19:28-42

Later, Joseph of Arimathea asked Pilate for the body of Jesus. Now Joseph was a disciple of Jesus, but secretly because he feared the Jewish leaders. With Pilate's permission, he came and took the body away (v. 38).

Joseph of Arimathea asked Pilate for Jesus' body. With the help of Nicodemus, he prepared the body for burial using strips of cloth and spices. When finished, they laid Jesus' body in a nearby tomb. It was probably very quiet while Joseph and Nicodemus fulfilled their task. No words were spoken. Perhaps their breathing was labored or their sighing deep as their fingers gently and tenderly wrapped the body of their friend. Maybe tears were shed in the stillness as grief filled their souls.

Joseph and Nicodemus were both members of the Sanhedrin and had been secret disciples of Jesus. Were they afraid of boldly stepping forward to care for Jesus' body? Were they remembering Jesus' teaching, his voice, his touch, or his many miracles? Or were they still stunned by the events of the day?

Regardless, these two men performed a great service in memory of the one who had changed their lives, given them hope, and loved them unconditionally. Jesus had touched their hearts and minds, and their lives were forever transformed.

All powerful God, you and you alone have the power to transform my life. I offer myself to you. Amen.

THURSDAY OF SEVENTH WEEK

Romans 10:8-13

If you declare with your mouth, "Jesus is LORD," and believe in your heart that God raised him from the dead, you will be saved. For it is with your heart that you believe and are justified, and it is with your mouth that you profess your faith and are saved (vv. 9-10).

Many people struggle with the divinity of Jesus and his victory over death. Some think that the resurrection was a hoax the disciples implemented to further promote the ideas of Jesus. Other criticisms question the idea of a power beyond what is seen. How can you believe in something that is not tangible?

Faith requires trust and propels us to believe that God exists even though we do not see him in a physical form. Faith is a process and offers us options that allow us to call upon a power greater than ourselves for answers and solutions. It gives us hope—hope that we can rise from the ashes of our lives, that we can change, that we can begin again, and that we can survive whatever life throws our way.

Although we did not witness the battle won on the cross, our faith persuades us to believe in this resurrecting power. In the middle of our struggles when God may seem absent, faith prompts us to believe that he is moving in us, around us, and through us. And it is through believing without seeing that we are transformed.

God of all creation, I believe that Jesus Christ is the Son of the living God and was raised from the dead through your resurrecting power. Amen.

FRIDAY OF SEVENTH WEEK

1 Corinthians 11:23-26

For I received from the LORD *what I also passed on to you: The* LORD *Jesus, on the night he was betrayed, took bread, and when he had given thanks, he broke it and said, "This is my body, which is for you; do this in remembrance of me." In the same way, after supper he took the cup, saying, "This cup is the new covenant in my blood; do this, whenever you drink it, in remembrance of me" (vv. 23-25).*

When Jesus gathered his disciples for the Last Supper, they probably were not fully aware of its significance. After witnessing the crucifixion, they would soon come to know its power and meaning.

Today, when we participate in the taking of communion, we are a part of the united body of Christ—a community of believers. Some of the principles of community include commitment, empathy, and trust. When we become a part of something bigger than ourselves, we learn to live in harmony and peace by respecting those around us.

In taking communion, our common bond is our belief in Jesus as the Christ and Son of the living God. Through our love and acceptance of one another, we all receive the opportunity to grow in our faith. In addition, we are equal around the communion table. Regardless of our backgrounds or circumstances, we are all seeking forgiveness, acceptance, kindness, happiness, success, peace, and love. When we take communion together, we become one with God and one another.

Holy God, when I take communion, may I be aware of the power and meaning of the new covenant through the body and blood of Christ. Amen.

Saturday of Seventh Week

2 Corinthians 5:20-6:10

We are therefore Christ's ambassadors, as though God were making his appeal through us. We implore you on Christ's behalf: Be reconciled to God. God made him who had no sin to be sin for us, so that in him we might become the righteousness of God (vv. 20-21).

Reconciliation is defined as the peace between humanity and God and is the center of the Pauline theology. Paul was aware that the purpose of Jesus' death and resurrection was to achieve an inner transformation in oneself—a new creation through faith in Jesus as the Christ. Paul's ministry of reconciliation was based on providing an example of love and forgiveness rather than dictating one to change.

When we come into relationship with God through our belief in the death and resurrection of Jesus Christ for humanity's salvation, we gain a harmony between our life and the inner reality of the Christ within. We then become willing to live as Jesus lived.

For Jesus, man's transformation was paramount to his ministry. He sought out the marginalized, the outcasts, and the weary and gave them a message of love, forgiveness, and hope. Through his resurrection, Jesus loosened the chains of death and gave us the reality of eternal life. Therefore, for those of us who believe, we are ambassadors for Christ and dedicated to sharing the message of hope to all in desperate need of a Savior.

God of hope and transformation, instill in me the desire to be your ambassador and share the message of hope through faith in Jesus Christ. Amen.

RESURRECTION...

rising again to life

EASTER SUNDAY

1 Corinthians 1:18-31

For the message of the cross is foolishness to those who are perishing, but to us who are being saved it is the power of God (v. 18).

The whole of Christianity hinges on the resurrection. When Jesus was crucified, he took on the ugliness of humanity and defeated the darkness in our lives. In that eternal moment of redemption, he disarmed everything of this world that claims authority over mankind. He gave us the chance for new life. He gave us the chance to begin again. He gave us hope.

Hope is that inherent force deep within us that propels us forward even when we are weary and burdened from the struggles of life. Against all odds, it calls us to see beyond the circumstances of our lives and to anticipate the remarkable. It is the power of change, and change is transforming.

For some, perhaps the message of the cross is foolishness or unbelievable. But for those who believe, we have the opportunity on this Easter morning to reaffirm our faith and belief in the risen Christ. The tomb is empty, and the resurrecting power of God is undeniable!

Holy God, I believe that the power of the resurrection is still available for me today and will transform my life. Amen.

REVELATION...

awareness of Christ with us

ROAD TO EMMAUS

Luke 24:13-35

Then their eyes were opened and they recognized him, and he disappeared from their sight (v. 31).

Often we do not see what is right in front of us. Two of the disciples were on their way to Emmaus, and a terrible sadness filled their hearts. A man approached them on the road, and they recounted all that had happened during the last few days. As the traveler walked with them, he related the Old Testament teachings which told of the Messiah's suffering. When they entered Emmaus, they asked the traveler to join them for the evening. As they gave thanks and broke bread, the eyes of the disciples were opened. The man was Jesus!

The disciples were so preoccupied and grief stricken that they failed to recognize the Christ. We often do the same. We focus on the busyness of life, obsess on our struggles and problems, and fall into the trap of despair. And in those moments, we do not have a clue who is in our midst.

Jesus made himself known to the disciples by speaking to their hearts. He speaks in the same way to us today. Even when we are unaware of his presence, he burns within us his message of love, forgiveness, peace, and victory.

Gracious and loving God, open my eyes to your presence in my life today. Amen.

THE MESSAGE...

sharing the good news

THE GREAT COMMISSION

Luke 19: 28-40

"Blessed is the king who comes in the name of the LORD! Peace in heaven and glory in the highest!" Some of the Pharisees in the crowd said to Jesus, "Teacher, rebuke your disciples!" "I tell you," he replied, "if they keep quiet, the stones will cry out" (vv. 38-40).

There is a fictional tale about Jesus returning to heaven after his time on earth. The angels gather around to hear his story. Jesus explains living among the people, teaching his disciples, expressing his love, and dying on the cross for humanity's sins. He also tells of his resurrection and announcing the coming of God's kingdom.

When he finishes, one of the angels asks, "What happens now?" Jesus answers, "Well, I left behind a handful of faithful men and women. They will tell the story! They will express the love! They will spread the kingdom!" Another angel asks "But what if they fail? What will be the plan then?" Jesus answers, "There is no other plan."

Like the disciples, we are called to tell the story, express God's love, and expand the kingdom. This is God's plan for each of us. "Go into all the world and preach the gospel to all creation" (Mark 16:15).

Almighty God, you have given me life and filled my life with your light, peace, and love. Empower me to share my experience, strength, and hope with those around me. Amen.

MATTHEW 28:20

And surely I am with you always,
to the very end of the age.

AFTERWORD

Lent provides us with a defined forty-day period of reflection on the life, death, and resurrection of Jesus Christ. Perhaps, during the last few weeks in the stillness of morning meditation, we came to know the Son of God in a new and exciting way. Through daily prayers, the resurrecting power of God may have been revealed to us as it had never been revealed before. Maybe, we felt God's presence in the deep recesses of our spirits. Whatever our individual experience during this forty-day journey of Lent, hopefully our relationship with God has grown beyond our previous understanding and has given us a new perspective of his presence in our lives.

Napoleon once said, "Everything in Christ astonishes me. His spirit overawes me, and his will confounds me. Between him and whoever else in the world, there is no possible term of comparison. He is truly a being by himself....I search in vain in history to find the similar to Jesus Christ, or anything which can approach the gospel. Neither history, nor humanity, nor the ages, nor nature, offer me anything with which I am able to compare it or to explain it. Here everything is extraordinary."

This Lenten season has come to an end. As we go forward in our discipleship, God's spirit will lead and empower us to share our experience, strength, and hope. For over 2,000 years God, as revealed through Christ, has changed millions upon millions of lives. And although at times we may have doubted his existence, challenged his authority, and felt unworthy of his love, he extends his grace to each of us still today.

When we open our minds and hearts to the presence of God, the spirit of the Son is made known within us. When we allow him to transform us, we become testaments to God's resurrecting power as revealed in our daily lives. And when we proclaim our faith in the risen Christ, we become followers of someone remarkable—a Savior for all mankind.

ABOUT THE AUTHOR

Sheri A. Sutton is an author, devotional writer, and poet. Her third book, *In Remembrance of Me,* is a collection of meditations for the season of Lent. In addition, her devotional writing has been published in the *Secret Place* devotional magazine and the *Lenten Devotions on the Lord's Prayer.*

As a member of the Wichita Falls Poetry Society and the Poetry Society of Texas, Sutton has been recognized in various contests. Her poetry has been published in the *Wichita Falls Literature and Art Review* magazine, The Poetry Society of Texas' *A Book of the Year,* and *Lifting the Sky.*

For a limited time, she wrote a monthly newspaper column while serving on the Community Editorial Board of the Times Record News.

Sutton also offers professional services that include writing and editing for books, newsletters, and other materials for individuals, companies, or organizations. Visit her website, www.sheriasutton.com, for more information.

Sutton and her husband, Lloyd Mark Sutton, live in Wichita Falls, Texas.